Dedicated to my **Moose** and my **Bug**. Never give up on your dreams. Work hard and believe in yourself. Then, like Jax, your dreams will take flight.

The Adventures of Wyatt and Friends: Jax Learns To Fly

Library of Congress Control Number: TXu- 2-312-754
ISBN-13: 9798218008703

Printed in the United States

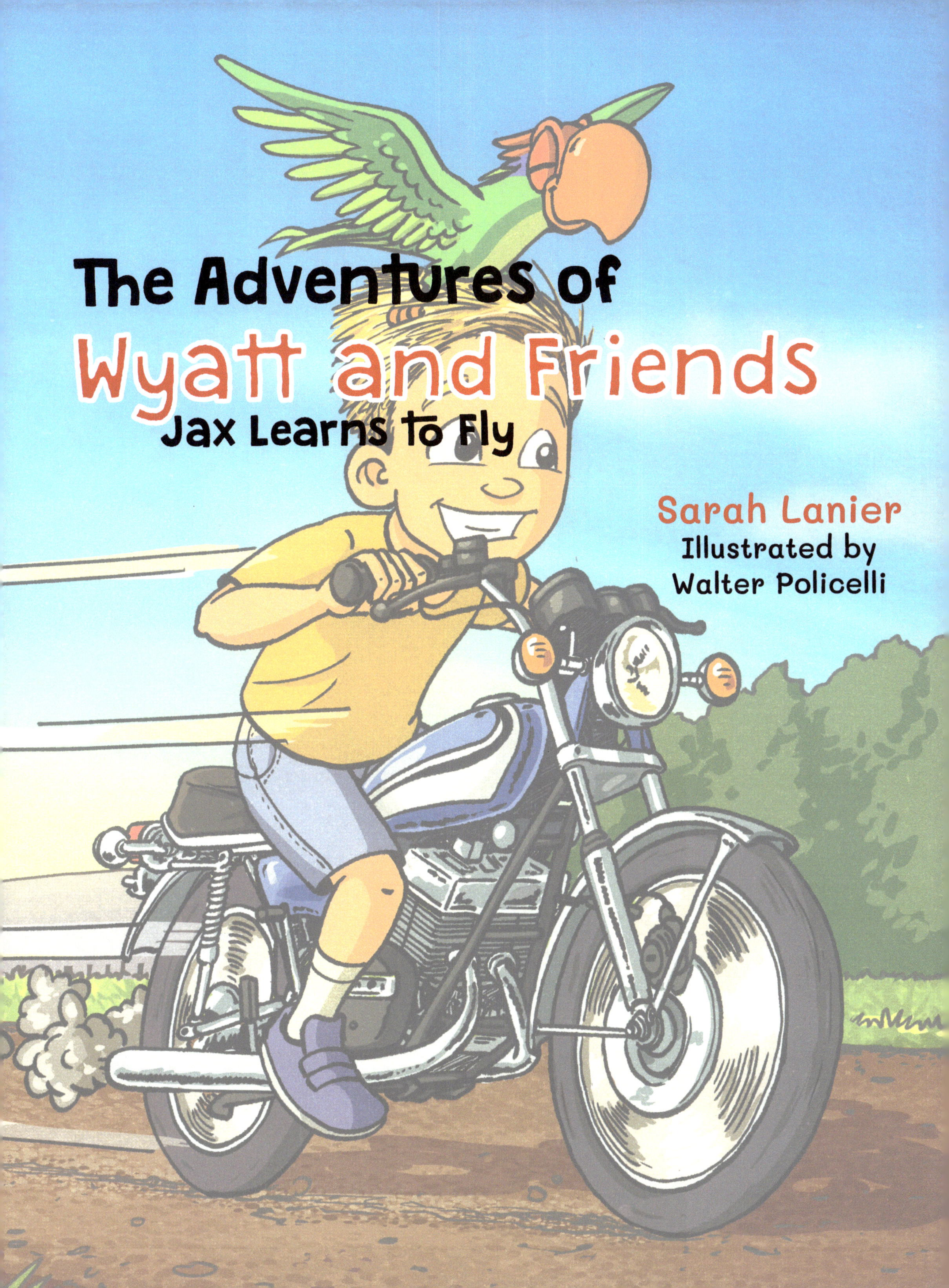

The Adventures of
Wyatt and Friends
Jax Learns to Fly
Sarah Lanier
Illustrated by
Walter Policelli

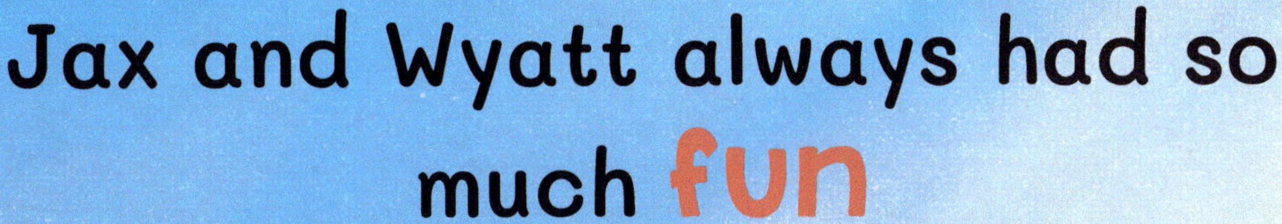

Jax and Wyatt always had so much **fun**

They played outside where they liked to **run**.

Saa
COOKIES
SUPER
MASON

Jax was a bird but she
still couldn't **fly**.

She thought she was
ready but was too
afraid to **try**.

Her best friend Wyatt and Rio the **horse**

said, "Dont worry Jax. We can help you, of **course**!"

First, Wyatt lifted
Jax way up high

Then pushed his friend up with a jolt toward the sky.

But that didn't work as Jax
quickly tumbled **down**

"Let's try something
else," the bird said with a
frown.

Next, they thought Rio could give Jax a **ride**

So they sat Jax upon the big horse's **backside**.

Jax said, "RUN RIO",
her wings started to
spread

But Rio was too bouncy,
so Jax fell on her **head**.

She was feeling quite tired
and she wanted to quit

But Wyatt said "come on Jax,
I know you can do it!"

So this time Jax sat atop little Wyatt's head

"Just close your eyes.
Spread your wings,"
Wyatt said.

Wyatt sat on his motorcycle and then he drove **fast**

"Are you ready to flap those wings?" Wyatt **asked**

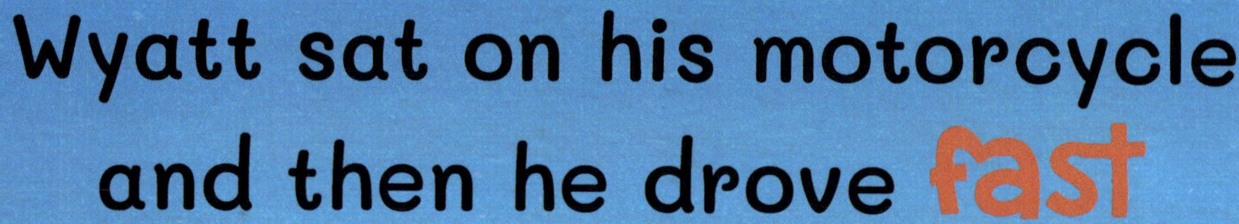

Jax felt the wind in her feathers,
then opened her eyes

She had finally done it!
She was soaring the skies!

She flew to the left and
she flew to the right
BELIEVE IN YOURSELF

She flew through
the clouds, and she
flew past a kite
SABRINA
SHANE

Wyatt and Rio cheered from down on the
ranch

Then Jax landed safely
on a nearby tree
branch

She said "thank you for helping me to finally soar"

And Wyatt replied,
"no problem! That's what
friends are **for**!"

Photos by: Tara Sproc Photography

The charismatic characters of this book are based on a real family that started an animal rescue ranch. When Nick and Steve (Daddy and Papa) adopted baby Wyatt, they decided to move to Texas and start a non-profit animal rescue called "Wyatt's Second Chance Ranch."

The ranch is now home to over fifty rescued animals, including emus, horses, goats, dogs, cats, parrots, pigs, chickens, and more! The ranch provides rescue animals with meals, medical care, grooming needs, plenty of cuddles, and a lifelong loving family. A portion of the proceeds from the sales of this book goes to support Wyatt's Second Chance Ranch and the animals' everyday needs. Thank you for your support!

If you would like to donate to Wyatt's Second Chance Ranch, you can do so by visiting paypal.me/wyattssecondchanceranch

About the Author

Sarah Lanier is a California native living in Kansas. Thanks to her hard-working husband, she is able to spend her days as a stay-at-home mom to her two beautiful and energetic children, playing and writing to her heart's content.

For more updates from the author, follow her across all social media platforms at @theesarahlanier

www.ingramcontent.com/pod-product-compliance
Lightning Source LLC
Chambersburg PA
CBHW042051100726
47973CB00014B/219